Songs Amongst Shadows

Anetta Fihnbrook

BookLeaf Publishing

India | USA | UK

Songs Amongst Shadows © 2024 Anetta
Fihnbrook

All rights reserved.

No part of this publication may be
reproduced, stored in a retrieval system, or
transmitted, in any form or by any means,
electronic, mechanical, photocopying,
recording or otherwise, without the prior
written permission of the presenters.

Anetta Fihnbrook asserts the moral right to
be identified as author of this work.

Presentation by *BookLeaf Publishing*

Web: www.bookleafpub.com

E-mail: info@bookleafpub.com

ISBN: 9789363315389

First edition 2024

My Request of Death

Take care of him
When you steal him away
Carry him gently
Beyond the light of day
Pierce not his back
With your skeletal hand
Just carry him gently
When departing our land

Take care of him
For I know he must go
I see it in his eyes
You needn't tell me so
I see how infection
Intertwines him with you
You terrible shadow
Who picks blooms in our meadow

So take care of him
When you steal him away
I beg you carry him gently
Though I know even then
You still will hurt me

If I Spend Spring In Grief

Don't make this goodbye!
I know you must go
But they say it's forever
Tell me that's not so
I could bear winter frosts
While you are away
For bleak, barren fields
Match my heart's decay
But I beg you, return
When the birds start to sing
For green shoots of life
Bring a sharper sting

How dare Mother Nature
Shoot up strong and sound
When she knows you lay cold
Six feet under the ground?
The world ought to slumber
By your side without sound
Shrouded in mourning
Till I hear you're home bound
They say you won't come
But that can't be true
And I'll wait till you're home
To sow seeds anew

I'm Fine, How Are You?

Help
Can't they hear me screaming?
I'm not okay, not today
I wish I could give up, decay.
Help
I think the world is crashing in
But I only let myself grin
Help
Can't they see my splitting skin
The secrets oozing from within?
Help
My tears roll down my face
But when they look I soon erase
The trace of pain upon my face.
Help
Why don't I let them see
How deep I dig my agony?
At the thought I flee
Help
Save me from this living hell!
I drown although I dug the well
Help
I don't think anybody hears
And I do not see any cures
And I'm surrounded by my fears

Help
The world is deaf, the world is blind
And I made myself hard to find
Please help

The Shadow's Lullaby

You are happy
You are safe
But there lurks something
You won't face

Run upstairs
Shut the door
So you won't see it
Anymore

Turn the lock
Hide the key
But that won't keep you safe
From me

I'm the shadow
I'm your fear
You can't lock me
Out of here

I live upstairs
In your head
Living off of
What you dread

I am here
You don't feel safe
You'll have to put me
In my place

Planting Poppies

I carved red rivers
To let the sorrow escape
From beneath my flesh.
I sowed the seeds,
Watched a feild of poppies
Bloom at my wrists.
Scarlet petals slipped away,
Staining my skin.
I have reaped
A hideous crop
Yet I plant again.
Here I am plowing furrows
In the fragile field,
Sowing the seeds.
I dig deep into the earth,
Drawing dark water
From the depths of the well.
Wine red, it floods the feild:
Running down my wrists,
Leaving red rivers
In its wake.

The Realization

Echoes of your voice resound
Promising that's you're homebound
Yet your chair sits empty there
Falling into disrepair

Your newspaper is at you desk
With your glasses, picturesque
But its date is weeks too old
And thick dust lays in its fold

You must be at coffee then
You'll be home before it's ten
Somehow the hour passes by
You're never late, I start to cry

I smell your cologne in the hall
Yet the illusion starts to fall
The horrid truth begins to call
And from your warm embrace I fall

Orange Tree

On a sunny day,
He picks oranges and gardens.
My world is at peace.

Was that a shadow?
Ignore it, pick the oranges.
He cares for his tree.

He must stay in bed.
Now his orange tree is alone.
He will garden soon.

Grey walls surround him.
He misses the orange tree.
A monitor beeps.

The tree starts to wilt,
But he cannot return yet.
Grandpa, please come home.

I Will Hold You In My Heart

I will enshrine you in my mind:
Your soft and crooked loving smile
The laughter that danced in your eyes
The dimples hinting at your glee
Your calloused hands, so hard working.
Every line that traced your face,
Can I memorize the map they made?
Can you be memorized?
How could I let you be confined?
You are- were- too alive
To be shrunken down to rote facts;
I cannot memorize you.
I cannot lose you.
So I will hold you in my heart
And your love will live in me.

Whispers in the Wind

I hear them on a stormy day
Intelligible, weighed with dismay,
Faintly crying far away
Mourning for they could not stay.
Golden roads led them astray
To the night where they decay.
Doomed, their bones crumble away
Turning flesh into gaunt grey.
Though their bodies life betray
Night cannot take their souls away;
They cling to light in this small way,
Yearning for life, trapped halfway.
So in the wind their whispers stay
Praying to be heard someday.

Shopping Spree

I catch a glimpse of myself
In the window at the mall
I'm in a blue mini dress
Bightly patterned
Daringly short
Carelessly cinched at my waist
With a satin scarf
Floral print
Alive
Who is this girl in the window?
She exudes joy
Radiates bliss
She's wearing pink lip gloss
Matching blush
She did not cry off her makeup
In the car
30 minutes ago
Sobbing hysterically
Barely able to see
Past the steering wheel
Gasping for air
Missing him
No
Dopamine radiates
Off her satin scarf

I hate that floral scarf
It looks alive
While he is dead
And I am lost
And there is nothing
All this
As I catch a glimpse
Of myself in the window
Is really just one thought
Simple
Practical
But it weighs down my chest
I need to buy more black

Goodbye

Goodbye
A short word really
Simply seven letters:

G is for your grey eyes
Grey fog swirling
Over the pier
Its sharp ocean scent
That follows you home
When you've been fishing
And your eyes twinkle
As you recount your day

O is for the old oak tree
Standing proud
Watching over your home
We raked up its leaves
Together
And you laughed
When I jumped in the pile
And I did it again
And again
To hear you laugh

O is for only
I've only loved you 18 years
Only my whole life
The doctor says you only
Have one to three months
Only a handful of weeks
How can it be
It can only be impossible

D is for dreams
You've listened to mine
So patiently
As they change
Time and time again
Artist, Actress, Anything
You say I could be anything
You mean it
You dream with me

B is for your blue shirt
It's your favorite
Its faded checkers
Smile at me from our photos
When I imagine you
You're in your blue shirt
The one that's so old
They tell you to donate it
But you never do
Because you love it

Y is for the yellow canoe
We rent every summer
Rowing together until
You stop halfway through
Too see if I'll notice
I laugh when you trick me
Your eyes twinkle back
You always save your jokes
For the people you love

E is for end
This can't be the end
Please
I'll miss you too much
Life without you
Is not life at all
This can't be the end

Goodbye
A short word really
Simply seven letters
Seven letters will end everything
All those days on the pier
All the laughter in your eyes
All our long conversations
All of you
Seven letters will steal you
It is impossible

You close your eyes
Our last goodbye
Goodbye

A Thousand Wishes

Dandelion
Make a wish
Please get well
Birthday cake
Make a wish
Please get well
Shooting star
Make a wish
Please get well
Prayer request
Make a wish
Please get well
A thousand wishes
Shining bright
Protecting you
Every night

Time of death 10:35

I believed in wishes once
Put my faith in something bright
Now I watch my wishes die
One by one, until no light

Thinking of You

I think of you during sunset
The sun dies every evening
But it's always reborn come dawn
Its homecoming is radient
It bursts over the horizon
Wrapping the world in its warmth
Returning in splendor
I don't care if you return with radience
I don't need splendor or show
Come home however you like
Just don't let this sunset be your last

Peace

Away into the sky I fly
Leaving my sorrows and worries behind
Living in a lullaby
Whose seams are made of dreams
My heart soars light
Untethered from terror, free from fright
Whatever happens
Whatever may be
The moonlight washes it over me
Baptized with peace, I levitate
Unfurling my wings, accepting my fate

Lighthouse

I decided to go to the beach
Let the waves wash me away
Let the sea swallow me up
Take me somewhere far away
I wished the waters would cradle me
Sing me a lullaby
I hoped they'd hold me close
When I began to cry
But I choked on the salt
It burned my lungs
The cruel current chained me
Oh what had I done?
But before the tides took me
A lighthouse shone bright
Spotting my misery in the night
It sent out a lifeboat
That threw me a rope
And so I was saved
By just one thread of hope

Stalking the Grim Reaper

Grim Reaper, I know that you're there
You can't hide from me
I spend all of my time grieving
And it makes you easy to see
I know you like to hide in shadows
But I'll grant you no privacy
After all that you've stolen
I'll never let you go free

Grim Reaper, where are you going?
You'll never escape from me
I'll stalk you from Heaven to Hell
Just to make you live in misery
Don't dare tell me I'm being unfair
After what you've done to me
A little discomfort is nothing
Compared to my agony

Grim Reaper, do you never grow tired?
You've been working for eternity
Your dark job seems rather unpleasant
It now occurs to me
Constantly bearing that bad news
Never once met with glee
Your gaunt face betrays your sorrow
I'm sorry you'll never be free

Guilty Rage

How can I be enraged
With He who is all good?
My own anger entraps me,
Betrays me as the villain
When my fury burns against Him.
Yet He stole you from me.
I wish my faith banished my fury
Yet my fury still persists
For I watched you waste away,
Your pain I can't forget.
In all His mighty mercy,
He let you writh in pain.
He laid His life down on the cross
And I know he owes us naught.
His glory reigns above us all
Yet your pain I can't forget.
My compassion feeds my rage,
My virtue turns to vice.
May He forgive my angry soul,
May He solve my plight.

Greif's Visitor

Hope is washed in by tides of tears
In the least expected years
When the world's shrouded in sorrow
She reminds us of tomorrow
She steps into the shrine of greif
To humbly provide relief
The shrieks and sobs do not repel her
For they have something to tell her
The desperate cries that echo there
Behind the dark shroud of despair
Point to darkness's bleeding heart
A lasting love, a subtle art
There loss and love are intertwined
Inseprable, they're hope defined
Love leads us to loss, to pain
Yet we choose it time again
That choice is hope personified
And she shall never be defied
So hope doesn't wipe away our tears
No, through them she gently peers
And sees the love rooted in tears

www.ingramcontent.com/pod-product-compliance
Lightning Source LLC
LaVergne TN
LVHW010533210726
843508LV00020BA/2969